Relationships Are Currency

Leveraging Social Capital to Build Wealth

Written and Produced by Greg Graham

Carmine Street Media Books

Written and Produced by Greg Graham

Published by: Carmine Street Media Books

Website: CarmineStreet.Media

Cover Design by: Jessica Jimenez

Dedicated to:

Every person who has enriched my life through the gift of genuine connection.

Table of Contents

Introduction:
The New Currency of Success

In an era where digital connections are abundant but meaningful relationships are increasingly rare, we need to fundamentally redefine what we mean by "wealth." Traditional metrics focus solely on financial capital—bank accounts, investments, and material assets. But this narrow definition fails to capture a crucial form of wealth that often proves even more valuable: social capital. This book presents a revolutionary perspective: your relationships are not just connections—they are a form of currency, often more valuable than the money in your bank account.

Think about the last time you needed to make something important happen. Perhaps it was landing a crucial meeting, getting a reservation at an exclusive restaurant, or finding the perfect candidate for a job opening. What made the difference? More often than not, it wasn't about how much money you could spend—it was about who you knew and, more importantly, who knew and trusted you. This is social capital in action, and when we begin to view wealth through this more holistic lens, we discover that true prosperity encompasses both our financial resources and the strength of our relationships.

The concept of relationships as currency isn't just a metaphor. Like financial currency, relationships can be:

- Earned through effort and investment
- Accumulated over time
- Spent wisely or squandered
- Invested for future returns
- Leveraged to create opportunities

- Used to access experiences and resources that money alone cannot buy

However, unlike traditional currency, relationship capital often appreciates with use. The more you thoughtfully engage your relationships, the stronger and more valuable they become. When combined with financial capital, these two forms of wealth can create a powerful multiplier effect, each enhancing the value of the other.

Drawing from decades of experience across multiple industries and continents, from the vibrant music scenes of Detroit, New York, Miami, and London to the innovative minds in Silicon Valley, from the United Nations to medical technology, I've witnessed firsthand how relationships can transcend traditional boundaries of industry, culture, and geography. What I've learned is that success in any field isn't just about what you know or even who you know—it's about how well you cultivate and maintain those relationships, and how effectively you combine your social and financial capital. As one music industry executive once shared with me:

"It's no longer what you know or who you know—it's *who knows you*."

Through practical frameworks, real-world examples, and actionable strategies, this book will teach you:

- How to build authentic relationships that create lasting value
- Why access and influence often matter more than traditional assets
- The critical difference between genuine relationships and superficial connections
- How to leverage social capital without depleting it

- Why relationships matter more than ever in our digital age
- The power of the "producer mindset" in relationship building
- How to create synergy between your financial and social capital

Whether you're an entrepreneur seeking to build your business, a professional looking to advance your career, or simply someone who wants to enrich their life through stronger connections, understanding relationships as currency will transform how you approach networking, professional development, and personal growth. Most importantly, you'll learn to see wealth in a new light—one that acknowledges the full spectrum of capital at your disposal.

Welcome to a new way of thinking about success—one where your relationship portfolio is recognized as an essential component of your total wealth, working in harmony with your financial assets to create opportunities and value that neither could generate alone.

In the chapters that follow, we'll explore how to build and maintain both forms of wealth, starting with understanding the fundamental shifts in how value is created and exchanged in today's social economy. We'll examine why traditional networking often falls short, and how to instead create authentic connections that generate real value for all parties involved.

This isn't just another book about networking—it's a universal guide to understanding and leveraging a more complete definition of wealth, one that recognizes relationships as a crucial form of currency in our time. Let's begin.

Acknowledgements

Immense gratitude to Dr. Emily Weil, Jessica Jimenez, Amon Focus, Anthony 'Tmor' Morris, Lisa James, Fred Solomon, Karen Lippe, Alex Cinus, Sharon Patin, Jasmine Star, Joshua Hodge, Chris Do, James Lilliewood, Dr. Mariajose Metcalfe-Lilliewood, Magen Connolly, Chadon Charles, Norm Escoffery, Laila Dolle, Gillian Barnes, Seref Mamas, Cyril Bizieau, Jeffrey Glenn, Sabrina Michelin, Gwen Gaydos, Baratunde Thurston, James Andrews

Special thanks to Alice Brito, Alanis Zalkind, Aisla Zalkind, Dr. Ted Graham, Carla Graham, Alexis Graham, Jillian Graham, Doug Graham, Janet Graham, Marty Smith and the entire Smith family, Dr. Kevin E. Potts, Ayesha Potts, Nechelle Vanias, Tony Vanias, Cassandra Trcka, Savannah Heathcote, Jayson Fittipaldi, Katy McCall, Jana Clarke, Ainsley Rodriguez, Nicole Del Busto, Liz Atlan, Geane Brito, Pete Werner, Jim Robinson, Marco Navarra, Marvin Coleman, Estela Rizzuto, Liane Ramirez-Swierk, Jeff Swierk, Hunter Lauten, Ainsley Lauten, Sheila Chang, Sébastien Rozec, Steven Aragona, Rachel Nunez, Vanessa Burgos, Marcus Ricketts, Jake Jackson, Bobby Hack, Irwin Hudson, Christopher Bass, Samuel 'Buzz" Thomas, Jalen Rose, David, Deana, and Lola Newman, Al Watson, George Lightbourn, Frank Jackson, Dr. Jason R. Brooks, Cecil Brown, Eric Rhea, Dr. Madalina Sucala, Rueben Hill, Kristian Hill, Dennis W. Archer Jr., Esq., Drs. Courtney and Carmen Hollowell, Dr. Christopher Hollowell, Dr. Sylvia Hollowell, Danielle Hollowell, Abby Steward and the entire Steward family,

Caralynn Brown, Aimee Burrell, Sheri Richardson, Carla Scofield, Dr. Patty Wong, Angie T. Giles, Steven Giles, Nicole Emiliani, Sam and Amber Prince, Jasmine Dotiwala, Shaista Niwaz, Selina Tobaccowala, Natalie Wade, Stephanie Haughton-Campbell, Tara Cowan, Kelvin Avon, Jennifer Chiang, Pia Wong, Birdie Lodders, Neil Brown, Hiromi Nakashimax Brown, Matt and Kate White, Natasha Brown, Dean Gardner, Ben Westwood, Richard Morris, Felix Pike, Laura Lafata, Corinna Moebius, Dana Brooks, Danyel Smith, Cal Newport, Chris Do, Matt Villacarte, Alex Farrace, Maureen McCormack, Chuck Vincent, Sunisa Nuonsy, Deena Sellers, Bonnie Blue Edwards, Thembisa Mshaka, Big Ced Thornton, Natalie Taguchi, Rory Platt, Ian Bassingthwaite, Regan Clark, Dan Klokow, Estela Romand, Lynell and Garland Doyle, Wil Van Zyl, Joanna Lawrence, Adrian Rezza, Lucas Rezza, Rashida Jones, Massita Montbrun, Briga Heelan, Emma Bunton, Jade Jones, Victoria and David Beckham, Tracey Wigfield, Katrina Bowden, Shizuka Anderson, Misako Envela, Christal Burnette

AI tools were used as resources to spell-check and sequence the author's original ideas and notes.

Using the *producer mindset* approach, this book was written and produced by
Greg Graham

Part I: Understanding the New Currency

Chapter 1: The Social Economy

Redefining Wealth Beyond Financial Metrics

As our world continues its quest to change rapidly, we need to fundamentally rethink our definition of wealth. While traditional metrics focus on monetary assets—bank accounts, investments, and material possessions—there's an equally powerful form of wealth that often goes unmeasured: the richness of our relationships.

Consider for a moment what truly opens doors in life. Is it always the size of your bank account? Or is it often who you know, who trusts you, and who's willing to vouch for your capabilities? In many cases, the strength of your relationships can create opportunities that money alone cannot buy.

The truth is, we're operating in a new kind of economy—one where social connections carry as much weight as financial transactions. This social economy runs parallel to our financial systems, often intersecting with and amplifying traditional forms of wealth, but sometimes completely transcending them.

The Intersection of Social and Financial Capital

The relationship between social and financial capital is complex and symbiotic. While financial wealth can certainly help create opportunities for building relationships, strong relationships can often lead to financial opportunities. This intersection creates what I call the "wealth multiplier effect."

Consider these real-world scenarios:

- A restaurant manager who cultivates strong relationships with regular patrons can maintain consistent business even on typically slow nights, creating financial stability through social connections
- An international business professional who maintains strong relationships across continents can create welcoming environments for meetings and negotiations, leading to more successful deals
- A well-connected individual might gain access to exclusive events or experiences that others can only access through significant financial expenditure

The key understanding here is that social capital isn't just an alternative to financial capital—it's a force multiplier. When you combine strong relationships with financial resources, each becomes more powerful. Your relationships can help you make better use of your financial resources, while your financial resources can help you create opportunities to build and maintain valuable relationships.

Why Relationships Matter More Than Ever

In our digital age, one might assume that traditional relationship-building has become less important. After all, we can connect with anyone around the world at the touch of a button. However, the reality is quite the opposite—relationships matter more now than ever before. Here's why:

The Trust Economy

In an era of information overload and digital noise, trust has become one of the scarcest and most valuable commodities.

Strong relationships built on genuine trust stand out in a world of superficial connections. When someone trusts you, they're more likely to:

- Share opportunities with you before they become public
- Recommend you to their own valuable connections
- Give you the benefit of the doubt in challenging situations
- Invest their time, energy, and resources in your success

The Power of Access

On many occasions, access to knowledge or relationships can have more impact than taking the time to accumulate all of the information on your own. Having the right relationships can grant you access to experiences, opportunities, and resources that might be impossible to obtain through financial means alone. Whether it's getting into an exclusive event, securing a crucial introduction, or gaining early access to opportunities, relationships often serve as the gatekeeper.

Global Connectivity

While technology has made it easier to connect with people worldwide, it has also made it more crucial to have genuine, meaningful relationships. In our globally connected economy:

- Business opportunities often cross cultural and geographical boundaries
- Success frequently depends on having trusted contacts in different regions

- Understanding different cultural contexts becomes invaluable
- Local relationships can have global impact

The Human Element

Despite (or perhaps because of) our increasingly digital world, the human element has become more crucial than ever. People crave authentic connections and value relationships that offer:

- Genuine understanding and empathy
- Real-world trust and reliability
- Personal attention and care
- Meaningful, shared experiences

Looking Ahead

As we continue to navigate this evolving social economy, understanding how to build and leverage relationships becomes increasingly crucial. The most successful individuals and organizations will be those who recognize that their network is not just a list of contacts, but a living ecosystem of relationships that needs to be cultivated, nurtured, and valued.

In the chapters that follow, we'll explore specific strategies for building your social capital, maintaining authentic relationships, and leveraging these connections ethically and effectively. We'll examine how to navigate the delicate balance between professional networking and personal connection, and how to ensure that your relationship currency maintains its value over time.

Remember: In today's world, your net worth isn't just about what's in your bank account—it's about the strength, depth, and quality of your relationships. Welcome to the social economy, where relationships truly are currency.

Chapter 2: The Anatomy of Social Capital

Defining Social Capital

Social capital, at its core, represents the collective value of your relationships and the resources they can mobilize. But unlike financial capital, social capital has unique properties that make it particularly valuable in the world today. It's not just about who you know—it's about the quality, depth, and reciprocal nature of those relationships.

Consider this analogy: If financial capital is like having money in the bank, social capital is like having a network of people who are willing to invest in your success. But there's a crucial difference—while financial transactions typically deplete resources, social capital often grows stronger with use. The more you thoughtfully engage your relationships, the more valuable they become.

The Components of Valuable Relationships

Understanding the anatomy of social capital requires examining the key components that make relationships valuable:

1. Trust

Trust is the foundation of all valuable relationships. In my experience across industries—from music production to technology, from international development to medical innovation—trust has consistently proven to be the most crucial element of social capital. Trust is earned through:

- Consistent reliability
- Transparent communication
- Following through on commitments
- Maintaining confidentiality when required
- Demonstrating genuine care for others' interests

2. Reciprocity

Valuable relationships are built on mutual benefit, but not in a transactional way. True reciprocity means:

- Creating value for others without immediate expectation of return
- Understanding and supporting others' goals
- Sharing opportunities and resources
- Being willing to help before you need help
- Celebrating others' successes

3. Accessibility

The value of relationships often lies in their accessibility when needed. This means:

- Being responsive within reasonable timeframes
- Making yourself available for important conversations
- Creating channels for efficient communication
- Understanding when to prioritize urgent requests
- Maintaining regular contact even when there's no immediate need

4. Depth

Surface-level connections rarely provide significant value. Deep relationships are characterized by:

- Mutual understanding of values and goals

- Shared experiences and challenges
- Personal investment in each other's success
- Understanding of each other's strengths and weaknesses
- Willingness to have difficult conversations when necessary

5. Authenticity

In an age of artificial connections, authentic relationships stand out. Authenticity involves:

- Being genuine in your interactions
- Showing vulnerability when appropriate
- Maintaining consistency between words and actions
- Sharing both successes and challenges
- Being honest about limitations and capabilities

Building Your Social Portfolio

Just as you would diversify a financial portfolio, building a strong social portfolio requires strategic thinking and deliberate action. Here's how to approach it:

1. Audit Your Current Relationships

Begin by assessing your existing relationships across different categories:

- Professional connections
- Industry contacts
- Cross-industry relationships
- Personal networks
- Community connections

2. Identify Gaps and Opportunities

Look for areas where your network could be stronger:

- Geographic regions you'd like to expand into
- Industries that complement your current focus
- Skills or expertise you'd like to access
- Demographic or cultural perspectives you're missing
- Levels of influence you'd like to reach

3. Strategic Relationship Building

Develop a plan for building relationships that:

- Aligns with your long-term goals
- Leverages your authentic strengths
- Creates value for others
- Builds diverse connections
- Maintains sustainable growth

4. Relationship Maintenance

Just as financial investments require maintenance, so do relationships:

- Regular check-ins without specific needs
- Sharing relevant opportunities or information
- Offering support during challenging times
- Celebrating successes together
- Providing value consistently

5. Leverage and Growth

Learn to ethically leverage your relationships while helping them grow:

- Make meaningful introductions between contacts
- Share opportunities that benefit multiple parties
- Create environments for collaboration

- Foster community among your connections
- Build reputation through reliable referrals

The Multiplier Effect

One of the most powerful aspects of social capital is its ability to create multiplier effects. When you connect valuable relationships with each other, you:

- Create new opportunities for collaboration
- Expand everyone's network exponentially
- Generate innovative solutions through diverse perspectives
- Build stronger communities
- Create lasting value for all parties involved

Looking Forward

Understanding the anatomy of social capital is just the beginning. In the chapters that follow, we'll explore specific strategies for building trust, maintaining authentic relationships, and leveraging your social portfolio ethically and effectively. We'll examine how to navigate different cultural contexts, use technology to enhance (rather than replace) real connections, and measure the return on your relationship investments.

Remember: Your social capital is a living, growing asset that requires attention and care. By understanding its components and deliberately building your social portfolio, you're investing in what might become your most valuable asset—your network of meaningful relationships.

The key is to approach relationship building not as a series of transactions, but as a process of creating lasting value for yourself and others. When done right, your social capital can become a self-reinforcing system that generates opportunities, insights, and value far beyond what any individual could create alone.

Chapter 3: The Currency of Trust

At the heart of every valuable relationship lies trust. While you can acquire financial currency through various means, trust can only be earned over time through consistent actions and authentic behavior. In today's digital age, where connections are abundant but genuine trust is increasingly rare, understanding how to build and maintain trust becomes a crucial skill.

Building and Maintaining Trust

The Foundation of Trust

Trust isn't something that can be rushed or manufactured. Like any valuable currency, it must be earned legitimately and maintained carefully. From my experience across multiple industries—from Detroit's music scene to Silicon Valley's tech corridors—I've observed that trust is built through:

1. Consistency in Actions

- Following through on commitments, no matter how small
- Maintaining the same level of reliability across all interactions
- Showing up when you say you will
- Delivering what you promise
- Being consistent in your values and behavior

2. Transparent Communication

- Being honest about capabilities and limitations
- Communicating challenges before they become problems

- Sharing relevant information proactively
- Admitting mistakes and taking responsibility
- Providing clear expectations

3. Demonstrated Competence

- Consistently delivering quality work
- Staying current in your field
- Understanding your limitations
- Knowing when to defer to others' expertise
- Continuing to learn and grow

4. Authentic Interest

- Showing genuine concern for others' success
- Listening actively and remembering details
- Following up on previous conversations
- Celebrating others' achievements
- Supporting during challenges

The ROI of Reliability

Understanding the return on investment (ROI) of trust helps us appreciate why it's worth the time and effort to build and maintain. The benefits of being trusted include:

1. Access to Opportunities

When people trust you, they're more likely to:

- Share opportunities before they become public
- Make valuable introductions
- Include you in important discussions
- Consider you for significant roles
- Invest in your ventures

2. Reduced Transaction Costs

Trust eliminates the need for:

- Extensive formal agreements
- Multiple layers of verification
- Constant monitoring
- Detailed documentation
- Excessive due diligence

3. Increased Efficiency

Trust enables:

- Faster decision-making
- Streamlined processes
- More effective collaboration
- Better resource allocation
- Quicker problem resolution

4. Enhanced Reputation

Being trusted leads to:

- Positive word-of-mouth
- Strong referrals
- Enhanced credibility
- Increased influence
- Better networking opportunities

Converting Trust into Opportunities

Trust, like any form of currency, gains value when it's properly invested and leveraged. Here's how to ethically convert trust into opportunities:

1. Recognition and Response

- Identify when trust has been established
- Understand the responsibilities that come with trust
- Recognize opportunities that trust enables

- Respond appropriately to trust-based opportunities
- Continue maintaining trust while leveraging it

2. Strategic Leverage

When you've earned trust, you can:

- Make meaningful introductions
- Propose collaborative ventures
- Suggest innovative solutions
- Share sensitive information appropriately
- Create value for multiple parties

3. Value Creation

Trust enables you to:

- Build larger networks through trusted referrals
- Create partnerships based on mutual trust
- Develop long-term relationships
- Generate compound benefits
- Establish lasting influence

Case Study: Trust in Action

Let me share a personal example from my time managing relationships at high-end venues. When venue owners and managers trusted me, it wasn't just about getting preferential treatment—it was about creating value for everyone involved. This trust allowed me to:

- Bring in reliable, high-value clients
- Create positive experiences for all parties
- Generate consistent business even on slower nights
- Make meaningful introductions between trusted parties
- Build lasting relationships that benefited everyone

The Multiplier Effect of Trust

One of the most powerful aspects of trust is its ability to create compound benefits. When people trust you:

1. They're more likely to trust those you recommend
2. Their trust in you extends to your other relationships
3. Your network becomes more valuable to everyone involved
4. Opportunities multiply through trusted connections
5. Your influence grows exponentially

Protecting Trust

Just as you would protect any valuable currency, trust requires careful protection:

- Never violate confidences
- Don't exploit trust for short-term gains
- Maintain professional boundaries
- Be careful with introductions and referrals
- Keep promises, no matter how small

Looking Ahead

As we move forward in this book, you'll see how trust forms the foundation for everything from building influence to creating opportunities. In the next chapter, we'll explore how to leverage this trust through the power of access—one of the most valuable benefits of strong relationships.

Remember: Trust is the hardest currency to earn and the easiest to lose. Every interaction either builds or diminishes trust. By understanding trust as a form of currency, you can make better decisions about how to earn it, maintain it, and convert it into opportunities that benefit everyone involved.

The key is to view trust not as a tool for manipulation, but as a precious resource that grows in value when properly cultivated and carefully protected. When managed well, trust becomes the foundation for all other forms of social capital.

Part II: Leveraging Social Capital
Chapter 4: The Power of Access

Our world is one where true exclusivity has become increasingly rare and valuable. While money can buy many things, there are doors that only relationships can open. This chapter explores how social capital transforms into tangible access and opportunities that often exceed what financial resources alone can provide.

Understanding Access as Social Currency

Think of access as an invisible key that unlocks experiences, opportunities, and spaces that aren't available to the general public. Unlike traditional currency, access through relationships can't be simply purchased – it must be earned through authentic connections and mutual trust. When you cultivate meaningful relationships, you're not just building friendships; you're creating pathways to experiences and opportunities that money alone cannot buy.

Consider how often you've heard someone say, "It's not what you know, but who you know." While expertise matters, relationships often serve as the bridge between capability and opportunity. In an age where information is ubiquitous, exclusive access has become one of the most valuable forms of social currency.

How Relationships Open Doors

Strong relationships create a ripple effect of opportunities. When someone in your network trusts and values you, they become invested in your success. This investment manifests in various ways:

- Direct introductions to key decision-makers
- Invitations to private events where meaningful connections happen
- Early access to opportunities before they become public
- Inside information about upcoming changes or opportunities
- Advocacy on your behalf in closed-door discussions

The key difference between trying to buy access and earning it through relationships is sustainability. Purchased access is typically transactional and temporary. Relationship-based access, however, tends to be ongoing and often strengthens over time.

When Social Capital Surpasses Financial Capital: The Story of Sarah Chen

Let me share the story of Sarah Chen, a first-generation immigrant who transformed her career through the power of relationships. Fresh out of college, Sarah worked as a barista at a high-end coffee shop in Seattle's tech district. Unlike her colleagues who saw it as just a job, Sarah made it her mission to learn every customer's name, their preferred drink, and small details about their lives.

One regular customer, David, always ordered a double espresso at 7:30 AM. Sarah noticed he often seemed stressed about upcoming presentations, so she started having his coffee ready when he walked in, along with a small note of encouragement. What Sarah didn't know was that David was a senior venture capitalist at a prominent firm.

When the coffee shop hosted a latte art competition, Sarah invited her regulars, including David. During the event, she mentioned her background in data analytics and her dream of working in tech. Two weeks later, David offered her an interview for an analytics position at his firm – a role that hadn't even been publicly posted. Despite having fewer technical credentials than other candidates, Sarah's demonstrated emotional intelligence and genuine relationship-building skills won her the position.

Fast-forwarding to today, Sarah leads the firm's data strategy team and has become known for her ability to connect with founders on a human level. Her story illustrates how authentic relationships can create opportunities that no amount of money or even traditional qualifications could secure.

The Hidden Economy of VIP Experiences: A Deeper Look

The hidden economy of access operates on principles that differ fundamentally from traditional markets. Understanding its unique characteristics is crucial for anyone looking to navigate this invisible landscape:

The Trust Matrix

Think of the hidden economy as a vast web of trust-based relationships, where each connection has four key dimensions:

- Depth of relationship
- Length of association
- Mutual value creation
- Network overlap

These factors combine to create what we call your "trust score" within any given network. The higher your trust score, the more doors open automatically.

The Currency of Reciprocity

Within this economy, reciprocity takes many forms:

- Knowledge sharing
- Emotional support
- Strategic introductions
- Opportunity creation
- Resource sharing
- Time investment

Unlike financial transactions, these exchanges aren't immediately balanced or quantified. Instead, they create long-term relationship equity that can be drawn upon when needed.

The Multiplication (or Multiplier) Effect

Perhaps the most powerful aspect of this hidden economy is its multiplication effect. When you provide value to one person, the benefit often spreads throughout their network, creating opportunities you couldn't have anticipated. This organic growth of influence is something money simply cannot replicate.

Navigating Exclusive Spaces: A Practical Guide

Successfully navigating exclusive spaces requires more than just getting your foot in the door. Here's a detailed framework for building and maintaining your presence in exclusive environments:

1. The Entry Phase

- Research thoroughly before entering any new space
- Identify and respect the unwritten rules
- Find a genuine connection or shared interest with existing members
- Enter through proper channels or introductions

- Stay humble and observant initially

2. The Integration Phase

- Contribute value before seeking benefits
- Build relationships horizontally, not just vertically
- Share knowledge and resources generously
- Respect confidentiality absolutely
- Develop your unique voice and perspective

3. The Establishment Phase

- Begin facilitating connections for others
- Create value for the community as a whole
- Develop your own sub-network
- Mentor newcomers who remind you of your earlier self
- Maintain authenticity as your influence grows

Common Pitfalls to Avoid

- Overemphasizing your achievements or connections
- Treating relationships transactionally
- Violating community norms or expectations
- Sharing access too freely or carelessly
- Listening with the intent to reply, not to understand
- Forgetting those who helped you along the way

The Art of Maintaining Access

Remember that maintaining access is often harder than gaining it initially. Key practices include:

- Regular, meaningful engagement with your network

- Consistent value creation for others
- Careful protection of trust and confidentiality
- Graceful handling of difficulties or conflicts
- Ongoing investment in relationship development

Looking Ahead

As we continue to explore the leverage of social capital, remember that access through relationships isn't about collecting powerful contacts or trading favors. It's about building genuine connections that create value for everyone involved. The most valuable doors are opened not by those with the most money, but by those who have earned trust and respect through authentic relationships.

In the next chapter, we'll explore how to transform these relationships into collaborative partnerships that can accelerate your success and create mutual value for everyone in your network.

Chapter 5: Network Effects

We often hear about network effects in relation to technology platforms—how each additional user makes the platform more valuable for everyone. But this same principle applies even more powerfully to human relationships. This chapter explores how to harness the exponential power of network effects in your professional and personal relationships.

The Multiplier Effect of Strong Relationships

Imagine throwing a pebble into a still pond. The initial splash creates ripples that expand outward, each ring affecting a larger area than the last. Strong relationships work in much the same way, but with an important difference: each "ripple" has the potential to create its own set of expanding circles of influence.

The Mathematics of Connection

While a linear network grows by adding one connection at a time, a well-cultivated network grows exponentially through what we call the "trusted introduction effect." Here's how it works:

1. First-degree connections: Your direct relationships
2. Second-degree connections: Your connections' connections
3. Third-degree connections: The connections of your second-degree network

Each strong relationship you build doesn't just add one person to your network – it potentially adds their entire network to your sphere of influence. This is why focusing on quality over quantity in relationship building can yield exponentially better results.

The Trust Cascade

When a trusted contact vouches for you, they transfer a portion of their social capital to you. This "trust cascade" can dramatically accelerate relationship building. Consider this example:

Maria, a marketing executive, spent years building a strong relationship with James, a venture capitalist. When James introduced Maria to Sarah, a startup founder in his portfolio, the introduction came with an implicit transfer of trust. What might have taken months to build from scratch was established in minutes through the power of a trusted introduction.

Cross-Industry Networking Strategies

While many professionals focus on networking within their industry, the most powerful network effects often come from building bridges between different sectors. This cross-pollination of ideas and opportunities can create unique value that others might miss.

The Power of Weak Ties

Research has shown that some of the most valuable opportunities come not from our closest connections, but from our "weak ties" – acquaintances who move in different circles than we do. These connections often provide access to information and opportunities that wouldn't be available within our immediate network.

The Story of the Conference Coffee Line

Take the story of Alex Patel, a UX designer who was standing in line for coffee at an AI conference. She struck up a casual conversation with the person behind her, Dr. Chen, about the frustratingly long wait times. This seemingly trivial interaction – a classic weak tie – led to an unexpected opportunity six months later.

Dr. Chen, who turned out to be a professor of computer science, remembered Alex's insights about user experience when his department was struggling with the interface design of a new AI research tool. What made this weak tie particularly valuable was that Dr. Chen operated in a completely different professional circle than Alex's usual network of tech startups and design agencies.

The resulting collaboration not only provided Alex with her first entry into academic research projects but also led to a series of speaking engagements at universities about the intersection of UX design and artificial intelligence. This opportunity would never have emerged from her strong ties, as her close connections were all in similar professional circles.

Strategic Cross-Industry Navigation

To effectively build cross-industry relationships:

1. **Identify Complementary Industries**
    - Look for sectors that interact with yours but aren't direct competitors
    - Consider industries that share similar challenges or customer bases
    - Find sectors that could benefit from your industry's expertise

2. **Create Connection Points**
    - Attend cross-industry conferences and events

- ○ Join organizations that attract leaders from multiple sectors
- ○ Participate in community or charitable initiatives that bring together diverse professionals

3. **Bridge Value Gaps**
    - ○ Identify areas where your expertise could solve problems in other industries
    - ○ Look for opportunities to connect people across sector boundaries
    - ○ Share insights that might be common in your industry but novel in others

Case Study: The Architecture of Cross-Industry Success

Consider the story of Marcus Rodriguez, a software engineer who built an extraordinary network across healthcare, technology, and finance. Rather than staying within the tech bubble, Marcus:

- Volunteered his technical expertise at a local hospital
- Joined a healthcare technology advisory board
- Participated in financial technology meetups

When the pandemic hit, Marcus's cross-industry network proved invaluable. He was able to:

- Connect healthcare providers with tech solutions
- Help fintech companies understand healthcare payment systems
- Facilitate partnerships between previously siloed industries

His diverse network allowed him to identify opportunities that others missed, ultimately leading to the creation of a successful healthcare payment platform.

Creating Value Through Network Synergies

The true power of network effects comes not just from having connections, but from creating value by connecting others. This is where relationship currency becomes truly multiplicative.

The Synergy Framework

To create lasting value through network synergies:

1. **Map Your Network's Assets**
   - Identify each contact's unique strengths and needs
   - Understand their goals and challenges
   - Keep track of their current projects and interests
2. **Spot Connection Opportunities**
   - Look for complementary needs and capabilities
   - Identify potential collaborative projects
   - Recognize shared challenges that could be solved together
3. **Facilitate Meaningful Connections**
   - Make strategic introductions
   - Create contexts for collaboration
   - Follow up to ensure value is being created

The Art of Network Orchestration

Becoming a network orchestrator or "superconnector"—someone who creates value by connecting others—requires:

1. **Deep Understanding**
   - Know your contacts well enough to predict what partnerships might work
   - Understand the timing of opportunities
   - Recognize when connections are ready to be made
2. **Strategic Timing**
   - Wait for the right moment to make introductions
   - Ensure all parties are positioned to benefit
   - Consider the long-term implications of connections
3. **Careful Facilitation**
   - Provide context for introductions
   - Help define initial collaboration parameters
   - Stay involved enough to ensure success without overstepping boundaries

Measuring Network Effect Success

Success in creating network synergies can be measured through:

- Number of successful collaborations initiated
- Value created for network members
- Strength of second and third-degree connections
- Reciprocal opportunities generated
- Long-term sustainability of partnerships created

Building Your Network Effect Strategy

To harness the power of network effects, develop a systematic approach:

1. **Audit Your Current Network**

- ◦ Map your existing connections
- ◦ Identify gaps and opportunities
- ◦ Assess the strength of various relationships

2. **Set Network Development Goals**
   - ◦ Define target industries for expansion
   - ◦ Identify key players you want to connect with
   - ◦ Set specific relationship-building objectives

3. **Create Value-Added Connections**
   - ◦ Look for opportunities to connect others
   - ◦ Track the results of introductions
   - ◦ Build systems for maintaining relationships

4. **Maintain and Nurture**
   - ◦ Regularly check in with key contacts
   - ◦ Update your network map
   - ◦ Measure and adjust your strategy

Practical Exercise: Network Mapping and Opportunity Analysis

The 30-Day Network Activation Challenge

This exercise helps you systematically identify and activate the hidden potential in your network.

Week 1: Network Audit

1. Create three lists:
   - ◦ Strong ties (people you interact with regularly)
   - ◦ Weak ties (acquaintances, former colleagues, friends of friends)
   - ◦ Dormant ties (previously strong connections that have faded)

2. For each person, note:
    ◦ Their industry/expertise
    ◦ Recent achievements or changes you're aware of
    ◦ Last point of contact
    ◦ Potential areas of mutual interest

Week 2: Gap Analysis

1. Create an "ideal network" map:
    ◦ Industries you want to connect with
    ◦ Types of expertise you need access to
    ◦ Geographic regions you want to reach
    ◦ Levels of seniority you want to connect with
2. Compare your current network to your ideal map:
    ◦ Identify gaps
    ◦ Look for weak ties who could help bridge these gaps
    ◦ Note strong ties who could make introductions

Week 3: Value Creation Plan

1. For each person in your weak ties list:
    ◦ Identify one specific way you could provide value to them
    ◦ Research their recent work or achievements
    ◦ Draft a personalized reconnection message
    ◦ Think of someone in your network they might benefit from meeting
2. Create a specific action plan for your top 5 priority connections:
    ◦ What value can you offer?
    ◦ What is your specific ask (if any)?
    ◦ What is the best medium for reconnecting?
    ◦ What is the ideal timing?

Week 4: Activation and Documentation

1. Reach out to one person each day:
   - Send your carefully crafted reconnection message
   - Share something of value (article, introduction, opportunity)
   - Make note of their response and any updates about their current work
2. Document results:
   - Track response rates
   - Note any surprising information learned
   - Record new opportunities discovered
   - List potential synergies identified

Follow-up Analysis

After completing the 30-day challenge, assess:

- Which outreach attempts were most successful?
- What patterns emerged in responses?
- Which value offerings resonated most?
- What unexpected opportunities arose?
- How many new connections were made through weak ties?

Use these insights to refine your network development strategy going forward.

Looking Ahead

As your network grows and strengthens, the compound effect of these relationships will create opportunities that would be impossible to generate alone. In the next chapter, we'll explore how to leverage these network effects to create sustainable competitive advantages in your chosen field.

Remember: The goal isn't to have the largest network, but rather to build a network that creates the most value for everyone involved. Focus on quality over quantity, and always look for ways to create synergies that benefit all parties involved.

Chapter 6: Relationship Quality vs. Quantity

Real Relationships in a Digital World

In an era where social media followers are often mistaken for influence and LinkedIn connections are confused with real relationships, understanding the difference between digital popularity and genuine social capital has never been more crucial. This chapter explores why quality beats quantity in relationship building and how to cultivate authentic connections in our increasingly digital world.

The Follower Fallacy: Why Social Media Numbers Don't Equal Influence

The Mirage of Digital Popularity

James Peterson had 100,000 followers on Instagram. His travel photos garnered thousands of likes, and his lifestyle appeared to epitomize digital success. Yet when he needed to raise seed funding for his startup, he discovered that his substantial digital following translated into zero meaningful investor connections. Meanwhile, Sarah Chen, whom we met in Chapter 4, with her modest 500 LinkedIn connections, secured funding through just three phone calls to her genuine professional relationships.

This stark contrast illustrates what we call the "Follower Fallacy" – the mistaken belief that digital popularity equates to real-world influence.

Understanding True Influence

Real influence operates on three levels:

1. **Access** - The ability to reach decision-makers directly
2. **Trust** - The confidence others have in your word
3. **Action** - The capacity to mobilize people to take meaningful steps

Consider these metrics:

- 10,000 followers might see your post
- 100 connections might engage with it
- 1 real relationship might actually take action to help you

The Mathematics of Meaningful Engagement

Research shows that human beings can maintain only about 150 meaningful relationships (Dunbar's Number). Within these:

- 5-15 are intimate relationships
- 50-60 are close friends/colleagues
- The remainder are casual but real connections

This biological limit suggests that anyone claiming to maintain genuine relationships with thousands of people is likely confusing visibility with connection.

Distinguishing Between Digital Connections and Real Relationships

The Relationship Authenticity Matrix

To evaluate the quality of your professional relationships, consider these dimensions:

1. **Depth of Interaction**
   - Digital: Likes, comments, shares

- Real: Personal conversations, shared experiences, mutual support

2. **Reciprocity**
   - Digital: Following each other, occasional engagement
   - Real: Mutual investment in success, active value exchange

3. **Trust Level**
   - Digital: Public reputation
   - Real: Personal vouching and risk-taking

4. **Access**
   - Digital: Through public channels or platforms
   - Real: Direct, personal contact information

Case Study: The LinkedIn Paradox

Consider the story of Michael Torres, a sales executive who conducted an enlightening experiment. He had 5,000+ LinkedIn connections and decided to test their value by sending two different messages:

1. A public post asking for job recommendations:
   - Received 200+ likes
   - 50 comments
   - Zero actual referrals

2. Personal messages to 20 people he'd maintained real relationships with:
   - 15 responses

- 8 direct introductions
- 3 job interviews

The lesson? A smaller number of authentic relationships generated more tangible results than thousands of digital connections.

Building Authentic Relationships in an Era of Surface-Level Networking

The Depth-First Approach

Instead of pursuing breadth of connections, focus on depth with select individuals:

1. **Identify Key Relationships**
   - Look for mutual interests and values
   - Focus on long-term potential
   - Seek complementary skills and networks

2. **Invest Meaningfully**
   - Schedule regular one-on-one time
   - Share vulnerable moments and challenges
   - Offer help without expectation of return

3. **Maintain Connection Quality**
   - Keep detailed notes on important conversations
   - Remember personal details
   - Follow up on discussed items

Digital Tools for Deeper Connections

Use technology to enhance, not replace, real relationships:

1. **Relationship Management Systems**
   - Track important dates and follow-ups
   - Note key personal information
   - Set regular check-in reminders

2. **Meaningful Digital Interactions**
   - Share personalized, relevant content
   - Engage in private conversations
   - Use video calls for face-to-face connection

The Art of Converting Digital to Real

Transform surface-level digital connections into meaningful relationships:

1. **Identification Phase**
   - Look for consistent, thoughtful engagement
   - Notice shared interests and values
   - Observe how they interact with others

2. **Transition Phase**
   - Move conversations to private channels
   - Share more personal insights
   - Suggest real-world meetings when possible

3. **Deepening Phase**
   - Create shared experiences
   - Introduce to your trusted network
   - Collaborate on meaningful projects

The Limitations of Digital Fame

Understanding the Digital Ceiling

Digital popularity has inherent limitations:

- Attention without action
- Visibility without vulnerability
- Reach without resonance

The Real Power of Genuine Relationships

Authentic relationships provide:

1. **Emotional Capital**

   - Support during challenges
   - Celebration of successes
   - Honest feedback when needed

2. **Professional Leverage**

   - Real opportunities
   - Meaningful introductions
   - Tangible support

3. **Long-term Value**

   - Sustained support
   - Growing trust
   - Compound benefits

Practical Exercise: Relationship Audit and Enhancement

Week 1: Digital Connection Assessment

- List your top 100 digital connections
- Identify those with potential for deeper relationship
- Rate current relationship depth (1-5)

Week 2: Conversion Strategy

- Select 10 connections to deepen
- Create personalized engagement plans
- Schedule one-on-one virtual coffee chats

Week 3: Relationship Investment

- Execute engagement plans
- Document responses and insights
- Adjust approach based on results

Week 4: Measurement and Adjustment

- Evaluate success metrics
- Document lessons learned
- Create long-term nurture plans

Looking Ahead

As we move forward in an increasingly digital world, the ability to build and maintain authentic relationships becomes even more valuable. In the next chapter, we'll explore how to leverage these genuine connections to create lasting impact and mutual success.

Remember: In the age of infinite connections, the scarcest resource is authentic relationship currency. Focus on building fewer, deeper relationships rather than chasing digital popularity. Your success will be measured not by how many people know your name, but by how many would take your call at 3 AM.

Part III: Strategic Relationship Building

Chapter 7: The Art of Cultivation

At its core, relationship cultivation is an art form that requires patience, intention, and genuine care. Unlike the instant connections promised by social media platforms, meaningful relationships that generate true social capital are cultivated over time through deliberate actions and authentic engagement.

Long-term Relationship Building Strategies

The most valuable relationships in your network will be those you've nurtured over years, not days. Building lasting connections requires a strategic approach that goes beyond the initial handshake or LinkedIn connection.

The Three Pillars of Long-term Relationship Building

1. **Consistency**
   - Regular, meaningful touchpoints
   - Following through on commitments
   - Maintaining presence during both successes and challenges
2. **Value Creation**
   - Identifying opportunities to contribute
   - Sharing relevant insights and resources
   - Making strategic introductions
3. **Authentic Interest**

- Understanding personal and professional aspirations
- Remembering important details
- Celebrating others' successes

Nurturing Professional Relationships

Professional relationships require a different approach than personal ones, but the fundamental principles remain the same. The key lies in finding the balance between professional boundaries and genuine connection.

Strategic Touchpoints

The frequency and nature of your interactions should align with the relationship's context and the other person's preferences. Consider these guidelines:

- **High-priority relationships**: Monthly meaningful interactions
- **Important industry contacts**: Quarterly check-ins
- **General network**: Bi-annual or annual reconnection

The Power of Contextual Communication

Your outreach should always have context and provide value. Examples include:

- Sharing relevant industry news
- Congratulating on achievements
- Following up on previous conversations
- Offering assistance with known challenges

Creating Win-Win Situations

The most sustainable relationships are those where both parties benefit. This doesn't mean every interaction needs to be transactional, but rather that the relationship should create mutual value over time.

Identifying Mutual Benefits

Before pursuing any relationship, ask yourself:

- What value can I bring to this person?
- What might they be able to offer in return?
- How can we create opportunities that benefit both parties?

The Reciprocity Matrix

Consider these four types of value exchange:

1. **Direct Exchange**
   - Immediate mutual benefits
   - Clear value proposition
   - Tangible outcomes
2. **Indirect Exchange**
   - Network introductions
   - Knowledge sharing
   - Future opportunities
3. **Compound Value**
   - Long-term collaborations
   - Building joint ventures
   - Creating shared resources
4. **Community Impact**
   - Industry advancement
   - Mentorship opportunities
   - Collective growth

Practical Implementation

To put these principles into action, consider implementing these strategies:

1. Relationship Audit

Conduct quarterly reviews of your key relationships:

- Assess the strength of connections
- Identify neglected relationships
- Plan strategic reconnections

2. Value Calendar

Create a system for regular value delivery:

- Schedule check-ins
- Plan content sharing
- Arrange face-to-face meetings

3. Opportunity Mapping

Regularly identify ways to create mutual benefit:

- Monitor industry trends
- Track others' goals and challenges
- Look for collaboration opportunities

Common Pitfalls to Avoid

1. **Over-automation**
   - Resist the temptation to automate relationship building
   - Personalization matters more than efficiency
2. **Inconsistency**
   - Avoid sporadic communication
   - Don't reach out only when you need something
3. **Superficial Engagement**
   - Go beyond surface-level interactions
   - Invest time in understanding others' needs

Looking Ahead

Remember that relationship cultivation is a continuous process that requires ongoing attention and care. The investments you make today in building and nurturing relationships will compound over time, creating a robust network of meaningful connections that can provide value for years to come.

Action Steps

1. Identify your top 20 relationships to cultivate
2. Create a relationship cultivation calendar
3. Develop a value-delivery system
4. Set regular review periods
5. Monitor and adjust your approach based on results

The art of cultivation is just that—an art. While these strategies provide a framework, success ultimately depends on your ability to genuinely connect with others and create lasting value in your relationships.

Chapter 8: Industry-Specific Relationship Building

While the fundamental principles of relationship building remain consistent across sectors, each industry has its own unwritten rules, cultural norms, and networking dynamics. Understanding these nuances is crucial for building effective relationships within specific professional contexts.

Service Industry Connections

The service industry thrives on personal interactions and word-of-mouth recommendations, making relationship building particularly crucial in this sector.

Key Relationship Dynamics

1. **Vertical Networking**
   - Building relationships with suppliers
   - Connecting with industry influencers
   - Developing relationships with critics and reviewers
2. **Horizontal Networking**
   - Establishing partnerships with complementary services
   - Creating referral networks
   - Participating in industry associations

Strategic Approaches

- **Regular Industry Events Attendance**
  - Food and beverage shows
  - Hospitality conferences
  - Service excellence workshops

- **Local Community Integration**
  - Chamber of Commerce involvement
  - Local business association participation
  - Community event sponsorship

Corporate Networking

Corporate environments require a more structured approach to relationship building, with careful attention to hierarchy and professional boundaries.

Internal Relationship Building

1. **Cross-Departmental Connections**
   - Building allies across different divisions
   - Understanding departmental interdependencies
   - Creating collaborative opportunities
2. **Vertical Relationship Management**
   - Developing mentor relationships
   - Building rapport with leadership
   - Nurturing relationships with direct reports

External Relationship Building

1. **Industry Peers**
   - Professional association membership
   - Conference networking
   - Industry-specific social events
2. **Stakeholder Management**
   - Investor relations
   - Client relationship management
   - Vendor partnerships

Corporate Networking Best Practices

- Maintain professional boundaries

- Document important interactions
- Follow up systematically
- Respect corporate communication channels
- Understand and adhere to company policies

Creative Industry Relationships

The creative sector values authenticity and innovation, requiring a more fluid and personal approach to relationship building.

Network Components

1. **Creative Collaborators**
   - Fellow artists and creators
   - Technical specialists
   - Production professionals
2. **Industry Gatekeepers**
   - Agents and managers
   - Gallery owners
   - Publishers and producers
3. **Support Network**
   - Critics and reviewers
   - Mentors and advisors
   - Industry advocates

Relationship Building Strategies

- **Portfolio Sharing**
  - Regular work-in-progress showcases
  - Collaborative projects
  - Open studio events
- **Community Engagement**
  - Artist collectives
  - Creative workshops
  - Industry showcases

Tech Sector Networking

The technology industry combines rapid innovation with strong community values, requiring a unique approach to relationship building.

Key Relationships

1. **Technical Community**
   - Developer networks
   - Open source contributors
   - Technical advisors
2. **Business Ecosystem**
   - Investors and VCs
   - Startup founders
   - Enterprise partners
3. **Industry Influencers**
   - Tech thought leaders
   - Industry analysts
   - Technical evangelists

Tech Networking Venues

- **Digital Platforms**
  - GitHub contributions
  - Stack Overflow participation
  - Tech-focused social media
- **Industry Events**
  - Hackathons
  - Tech conferences and facilitated discussions
  - Meetups and user groups

Cross-Industry Relationship Building

Identifying Common Ground

1. **Universal Needs**
   - Professional development

- Resource access
- Market insights

2. **Shared Challenges**
   - Regulatory compliance
   - Digital transformation
   - Talent acquisition

Building Bridges

- **Cross-Industry Events**
  - Innovation forums
  - Leadership conferences
  - Sustainability initiatives
- **Collaborative Projects**
  - Joint ventures
  - Research partnerships
  - Community initiatives

Practical Implementation Tools

Industry-Specific Relationship Management

1. **Relationship Mapping**
   - Industry influence matrix
   - Stakeholder analysis
   - Network gap assessment
2. **Communication Planning**
   - Industry-appropriate channels
   - Communication frequency
   - Content relevance

Measuring Success

1. **Industry-Specific Metrics**
   - Relationship depth
   - Network diversity
   - Engagement quality

2. **ROI Tracking**
    - Opportunity generation
    - Resource access
    - Knowledge exchange

Looking Forward

As industries continue to evolve and converge, the ability to build and maintain relationships across sectors becomes increasingly valuable. Success lies in:

1. **Adaptability**
    - Understanding industry-specific norms
    - Adjusting communication styles
    - Embracing new networking tools
2. **Authentication**
    - Maintaining genuine connections
    - Building trust across sectors
    - Creating lasting value
3. **Innovation**
    - Identifying emerging networking channels
    - Creating cross-industry opportunities
    - Developing new relationship-building approaches

Remember that while each industry has its unique characteristics, authentic relationship building remains the foundation of successful networking across all sectors. The key is to adapt your approach while maintaining your integrity and genuine interest in creating mutual value.

Chapter 9: The Ethics of Social Capital

In an era where connections can be commoditized and relationships monetized, maintaining ethical standards in relationship building has never been more crucial. This chapter explores how to build and leverage social capital while staying true to your values and maintaining authentic connections.

The Foundation of Authentic Relationships

Understanding Authenticity in Professional Contexts

Authenticity doesn't mean sharing everything or dropping all professional boundaries. Instead, it means:

1. **Genuine Intent**
   - Building relationships based on mutual interest and respect
   - Focusing on long-term value over short-term gain
   - Being honest about your capabilities and limitations
2. **Transparent Communication**
   - Clear communication about expectations
   - Honest representation of your role and influence
   - Open discussion about mutual benefits
3. **Consistent Behavior**
   - Alignment between words and actions
   - Reliable follow-through on commitments

- ◦ Consistent treatment of all network members

Avoiding Transactional Relationships

One of the biggest ethical challenges in building social capital is avoiding purely transactional relationships. While all professional relationships involve some element of exchange, purely transactional connections can be damaging to both parties.

Signs of Transactional Relationships

1. **Short-term Focus**
   - ◦ Interest only when immediate needs arise
   - ◦ Lack of investment in relationship development
   - ◦ Disappearance after needs are met
2. **One-sided Value Exchange**
   - ◦ Unbalanced giving and taking
   - ◦ Lack of reciprocity
   - ◦ Focus solely on personal gain
3. **Surface-level Engagement**
   - ◦ Minimal personal investment
   - ◦ Lack of genuine interest
   - ◦ Automated or templated interactions

Moving Beyond Transactions

1. **Value-First Mindset**
   - ◦ Give before expecting returns
   - ◦ Focus on creating mutual benefit
   - ◦ Invest in relationship development
2. **Long-term Perspective**
   - ◦ Build relationships before you need them
   - ◦ Maintain connections during good times
   - ◦ Invest in others' success
3. **Authentic Engagement**
   - ◦ Show genuine interest in others

- Share relevant experiences and insights
- Celebrate others' successes

Building Sustainable Networks

Sustainable networks are built on ethical foundations that can withstand the test of time and changing circumstances.

Core Principles of Sustainable Networking

1. **Trust-Based Foundations**
   - Building credibility through consistent actions
   - Maintaining confidentiality
   - Following through on commitments
2. **Mutual Growth**
   - Supporting others' development
   - Sharing opportunities
   - Creating collaborative environments
3. **Balanced Value Exchange**
   - Understanding each party's needs
   - Creating reciprocal opportunities
   - Maintaining fair expectations

Ethical Considerations in Network Building

1. **Privacy and Boundaries**
   - Respecting personal information
   - Understanding professional boundaries
   - Managing shared connections
2. **Power Dynamics**
   - Acknowledging hierarchical relationships
   - Using influence responsibly
   - Protecting vulnerable parties
3. **Cultural Sensitivity**
   - Respecting diverse backgrounds
   - Understanding cultural norms
   - Adapting communication styles

Navigating Ethical Challenges

Common Ethical Dilemmas

1. **Information Sharing**
   - What to share and with whom
   - Managing confidential information
   - Balancing transparency with discretion
2. **Competing Interests**
   - Managing multiple relationships
   - Handling conflicts of interest
   - Maintaining neutrality
3. **Obligation Management**
   - Setting appropriate expectations
   - Managing favors and returns
   - Declining requests gracefully

Ethical Decision-Making Framework

1. **Assessment Questions**
   - Is this action aligned with my values?
   - Would I be comfortable if this was made public?
   - Does this create mutual benefit?
   - Am I respecting all parties involved?
2. **Implementation Guidelines**
   - Document important decisions
   - Communicate clearly with all parties
   - Maintain consistent standards
   - Seek advice when needed

Maintaining Ethical Standards in the Digital Age

Digital Ethics Considerations

1. **Online Presence**
   ◦ Authentic personal branding
   ◦ Responsible content sharing
   ◦ Digital footprint management
2. **Virtual Networking**
   ◦ Building genuine connections remotely
   ◦ Managing online relationships
   ◦ Digital communication etiquette
3. **Data Privacy**
   ◦ Protecting contact information
   ◦ Managing shared data
   ◦ Respecting privacy preferences

Future-Proofing Your Network

Building Long-term Trust

1. **Reputation Management**
   ◦ Consistent ethical behavior
   ◦ Proactive problem resolution
   ◦ Transparent communication
2. **Network Maintenance**
   ◦ Regular relationship review
   ◦ Value renewal strategies
   ◦ Ethical engagement practices

Creating Ethical Legacy

1. **Mentorship and Teaching**
   ◦ Sharing ethical practices
   ◦ Guiding others in relationship building
   ◦ Leading by example
2. **Community Building**
   ◦ Fostering ethical networking environments
   ◦ Creating supportive communities
   ◦ Promoting best practices

Action Steps for Ethical Networking

1. **Personal Ethics Audit**
   - Review current relationships
   - Assess communication practices
   - Evaluate value exchange patterns
2. **Relationship Review**
   - Identify transactional relationships
   - Plan authentic engagement strategies
   - Develop value creation opportunities
3. **System Development**
   - Create ethical guidelines
   - Establish boundary frameworks
   - Develop communication protocols

Remember that ethical relationship building is not just about following rules—it's about creating genuine connections that benefit all parties while maintaining personal and professional integrity. The strongest networks are built on trust, authenticity, and mutual respect, making ethical considerations not just moral imperatives but practical necessities for long-term success.

Part IV: Maximizing Your Social Worth

Chapter 10: Measuring Relationship ROI

While relationships can't be reduced purely to numbers, understanding the value and return on investment (ROI) of your social capital is crucial for strategic network development. This chapter explores methods for quantifying, tracking, and optimizing the value of your professional relationships.

Quantifying Social Capital

Relationship Value Metrics

1. **Direct Value Indicators**
   - Revenue generated through referrals
   - Cost savings from shared resources
   - Access to opportunities
   - Time saved through network assistance
2. **Indirect Value Indicators**
   - Knowledge gained
   - Industry insights acquired
   - Brand enhancement
   - Reputation strengthening

Measurement Framework

1. **Relationship Strength Index (RSI)**
   - Frequency of meaningful interaction

- ◦ Depth of engagement
- ◦ Reciprocity level
- ◦ Trust quotient
2. **Network Quality Score**
   - ◦ Diversity of connections
   - ◦ Industry influence of contacts
   - ◦ Geographic reach
   - ◦ Access to decision-makers

Tracking Relationship Value

Systematic Monitoring

1. **Key Performance Indicators (KPIs)**
   - ◦ Number of meaningful interactions
   - ◦ Response rate to outreach
   - ◦ Referral frequency
   - ◦ Resource exchange rate
2. **Value Creation Metrics**
   - ◦ Opportunities generated
   - ◦ Knowledge shared
   - ◦ Problems solved
   - ◦ Introductions made

Tracking Systems

1. **Relationship Management Dashboard**
   - ◦ Contact frequency
   - ◦ Value exchange log
   - ◦ Interaction quality
   - ◦ Follow-up status
2. **Value Exchange Matrix**
   - ◦ Resources provided
   - ◦ Benefits received
   - ◦ Pending exchanges
   - ◦ Future opportunities

Identifying High-Value Connections

Connection Assessment Framework

1. **Strategic Value Analysis**
   - Industry influence
   - Decision-making authority
   - Resource access
   - Network reach
2. **Relationship Potential Score**
   - Growth opportunities
   - Mutual interests
   - Collaborative potential
   - Long-term alignment

Priority Matrix

1. **High-Priority Relationships**
   - Strategic importance
   - Current value delivery
   - Future potential
   - Engagement level
2. **Development Opportunities**
   - Emerging connections
   - Untapped potential
   - Growth trajectory
   - Resource requirements

ROI Calculation Methods

Quantitative Metrics

1. **Financial Returns**

   ROI = (Value Generated - Investment) / Investment x 100

- Direct revenue
- Cost savings
- Resource efficiency
- Time value

2. **Network Growth Metrics**

   __Network Growth Rate__ = (New Valuable Connections / Time Period)

   - Connection acquisition rate
   - Relationship depth progression
   - Engagement frequency
   - Value exchange rate

Qualitative Assessment

1. **Relationship Quality Indicators**
   - Trust level
   - Communication quality
   - Mutual understanding
   - Value alignment
2. **Strategic Impact Measures**
   - Industry influence gain
   - Knowledge acquisition
   - Opportunity access
   - Reputation enhancement

Investment Optimization

Resource Allocation

1. **Time Investment**
   - Relationship building activities
   - Maintenance requirements
   - Development opportunities
   - Recovery periods

2. **Resource Distribution**

   Efficiency Ratio = *Value Generated / Resources Invested*

   - ○ Contact prioritization
   - ○ Engagement planning
   - ○ Follow-up systems
   - ○ Value delivery methods

ROI Improvement Strategies

1. **Value Enhancement**
   - ○ Increasing engagement quality
   - ○ Expanding value exchange
   - ○ Developing new opportunities
   - ○ Strengthening connections
2. **Cost Reduction**
   - ○ Automating routine tasks
   - ○ Streamlining communications
   - ○ Optimizing touchpoints
   - ○ Leveraging technology

Practical Implementation

Measurement Systems

1. **Relationship Tracking Tool**
   - ○ Contact management
   - ○ Interaction logging
   - ○ Value exchange recording
   - ○ ROI calculation
2. **Progress Monitoring**
   - ○ Regular assessments
   - ○ Performance reviews
   - ○ Adjustment planning
   - ○ Goal tracking

Analysis and Optimization

1. **Regular Review Process**
    - Monthly value assessment
    - Quarterly relationship audit
    - Annual strategy review
    - Continuous improvement planning
2. **Optimization Framework**
    - Performance analysis
    - Strategy adjustment
    - Resource reallocation
    - Goal refinement

Future-Focused Metrics

Emerging Value Indicators

1. **Digital Influence**
    - Online engagement
    - Digital reach
    - Virtual networking effectiveness
    - Social media impact
2. **Innovation Potential**
    - Collaborative opportunities
    - Knowledge sharing capacity
    - Creative synergies
    - Development possibilities

Forward-Looking Analysis

1. **Trend Monitoring**
    - Industry developments
    - Relationship evolution
    - Value creation opportunities
    - Network growth potential
2. **Strategic Planning**

- Future value projection
- Development planning
- Resource allocation
- Goal setting

Action Steps

1. **Implementation Plan**
   - Set up tracking systems
   - Establish measurement criteria
   - Define success metrics
   - Create review schedule
2. **Optimization Strategy**
   - Identify improvement areas
   - Develop enhancement plans
   - Allocate resources
   - Monitor progress

Remember that while measuring relationship ROI is important, not all value can be quantified. Balance numerical metrics with qualitative assessments to maintain authentic connections while optimizing your social capital investment.

Chapter 11: Creating Social Wealth

Social wealth creation goes beyond simply maintaining relationships—it involves strategically building and leveraging your social capital to create lasting value for yourself and your network. This chapter explores comprehensive strategies for building, managing, and maximizing your social portfolio.

Strategies for Building Your Social Portfolio

Portfolio Diversification

1. **Industry Sector Balance**
   - Core industry connections
   - Adjacent sector relationships
   - Cross-industry alliances
   - Emerging market contacts
2. **Relationship Types**
   - Strategic partners
   - Mentors and advisors
   - Industry influencers
   - Rising stars
   - Operational contacts

Strategic Development

1. **Vertical Integration**
   - Senior leadership connections
   - Peer-level relationships
   - Emerging talent networks
   - Industry thought leaders

2. **Horizontal Expansion**
   - Cross-functional relationships
   - Geographic diversity
   - Cultural breadth
   - Skill set variety

Converting Relationships into Opportunities

Opportunity Identification

1. **Active Listening Framework**
   - Need recognition
   - Problem identification
   - Resource mapping
   - Solution matching
2. **Value Gap Analysis**
   - Market inefficiencies
   - Unmet needs
   - Resource misalignment
   - Collaboration potential

Opportunity Activation

1. **Connection Catalysis**
   - Strategic introductions
   - Resource sharing
   - Knowledge exchange
   - Collaborative projects
2. **Value Creation Process**
   - Identifying mutual benefits
   - Structuring partnerships
   - Developing initiatives
   - Measuring outcomes

Maintaining Long-term Relationship Value

Value Sustainability

1. **Continuous Value Creation**
   - Regular value assessment
   - Proactive opportunity identification
   - Resource optimization
   - Relationship evolution
2. **Investment Protection**
   - Trust building
   - Conflict prevention
   - Crisis management
   - Reputation maintenance

Growth Strategies

1. **Relationship Expansion**
   - Deepening existing connections
   - Exploring new dimensions
   - Creating joint ventures
   - Developing shared initiatives
2. **Value Multiplication**
   - Network effect leverage
   - Synergy creation
   - Resource multiplication
   - Impact scaling

Building Social Wealth Systems

Infrastructure Development

1. **Relationship Management Framework**
   - Contact organization
   - Interaction scheduling
   - Value tracking

- ◦ Follow-up systems
2. **Value Creation Platform**
   - ◦ Opportunity identification
   - ◦ Resource matching
   - ◦ Collaboration tools
   - ◦ Impact measurement

Automation and Efficiency

1. **Process Optimization**
   - ◦ Routine task automation
   - ◦ Communication templates
   - ◦ Follow-up systems
   - ◦ Resource scheduling
2. **Technology Integration**
   - ◦ CRM utilization
   - ◦ Communication tools
   - ◦ Project management systems
   - ◦ Analytics platforms

Maximizing Return on Relationships

Value Optimization

1. **Resource Allocation**
   - ◦ Time investment
   - ◦ Energy distribution
   - ◦ Asset deployment
   - ◦ Attention management
2. **Impact Maximization**
   - ◦ Strategic positioning
   - ◦ Influence leverage
   - ◦ Network effect
   - ◦ Value multiplication

Synergy Creation

1. **Collaboration Framework**
   ◦ Partnership development
   ◦ Resource sharing
   ◦ Knowledge exchange
   ◦ Joint ventures
2. **Network Effect Activation**
   ◦ Connection clustering
   ◦ Value chain integration
   ◦ Community building
   ◦ Impact scaling

Advanced Wealth Creation Strategies

Portfolio Enhancement

1. **Strategic Positioning**
   ◦ Industry leadership
   ◦ Thought leadership
   ◦ Innovation leadership
   ◦ Community leadership
2. **Value Chain Integration**
   ◦ Vertical integration
   ◦ Horizontal expansion
   ◦ Cross-sector collaboration
   ◦ Market penetration

Wealth Multiplication

1. **Leverage Points**
   ◦ Network effects
   ◦ Scale advantages
   ◦ Synergy creation
   ◦ Resource multiplication
2. **Impact Scaling**
   ◦ Influence expansion
   ◦ Value multiplication
   ◦ Reach extension

- ◦ Depth enhancement

Future-Proofing Social Wealth

Adaptability Planning

1. **Trend Monitoring**
   - ◦ Industry evolution
   - ◦ Technology changes
   - ◦ Social shifts
   - ◦ Market dynamics
2. **Strategic Flexibility**
   - ◦ Relationship adaptation
   - ◦ Value proposition evolution
   - ◦ Resource reallocation
   - ◦ Strategy adjustment

Innovation Integration

1. **Emerging Opportunities**
   - ◦ New technologies
   - ◦ Market changes
   - ◦ Social shifts
   - ◦ Value creation models
2. **Development Areas**
   - ◦ Skill enhancement
   - ◦ Knowledge acquisition
   - ◦ Capability building
   - ◦ Resource development

Action Steps for Wealth Creation

1. **Portfolio Assessment**
   - ◦ Current state analysis
   - ◦ Gap identification
   - ◦ Opportunity mapping
   - ◦ Strategy development

2. **Implementation Plan**
    ◦ Priority setting
    ◦ Resource allocation
    ◦ Timeline development
    ◦ Progress monitoring
3. **Optimization Process**
    ◦ Regular review
    ◦ Strategy adjustment
    ◦ Resource reallocation
    ◦ Impact assessment

Remember that creating social wealth is a dynamic process that requires continuous attention, adaptation, and innovation. Success comes from building authentic relationships while strategically positioning yourself to create and capture value within your network.

Chapter 12: Future of Social Capital

As we advance into an increasingly connected world, the nature and value of social capital continues to evolve. Understanding emerging trends and preparing for the next evolution of social currency is crucial for maintaining and growing your network's value in the years ahead. The ideas discussed below will likely become more prominent.

Emerging Trends in Networking

Digital Transformation

1. **Virtual Relationship Building**
   - Immersive networking platforms
   - Virtual reality meetups
   - Digital relationship management
   - Remote collaboration tools
2. **AI-Enhanced Networking**
   - Intelligent relationship matching
   - Predictive networking opportunities
   - Automated value identification
   - Smart relationship maintenance
3. **Web3 and Decentralized Networks**
   - Blockchain-verified relationships
   - Token-based trust systems
   - Decentralized reputation networks
   - Smart contract collaboration

Social Evolution

1. **Global Connectivity**
   - Cross-cultural networking
   - International relationship building

- ◦ Global value creation
- ◦ Borderless collaboration
2. **Generation Z Influence**
   - ◦ New communication norms
   - ◦ Value-driven relationships
   - ◦ Purpose-aligned networking
   - ◦ Social impact focus

Technology and Relationship Building

Emerging Technologies

1. **Artificial Intelligence**
   - ◦ Relationship analytics
   - ◦ Network optimization
   - ◦ Communication enhancement
   - ◦ Value prediction
2. **Extended Reality (XR)**
   - ◦ Virtual networking spaces
   - ◦ Augmented relationship data
   - ◦ Immersive collaboration
   - ◦ Mixed reality meetings
3. **Blockchain and Web3**
   - ◦ Trust verification
   - ◦ Value exchange protocols
   - ◦ Decentralized identity
   - ◦ Smart relationship contracts

Digital Integration

1. **Platform Evolution**
   - ◦ Integrated relationship management
   - ◦ Cross-platform synchronization
   - ◦ Unified communication systems
   - ◦ Value tracking platforms
2. **Data-Driven Networking**
   - ◦ Relationship analytics

- ◦ Network optimization
- ◦ Value measurement
- ◦ Impact assessment

How Can We Prepare for this Next Evolution?

Skill Development

1. **Digital Literacy**
   - ◦ Platform proficiency
   - ◦ Technology adoption
   - ◦ Digital communication
   - ◦ Virtual collaboration
2. **Future-Ready Capabilities**
   - ◦ Cross-cultural competence
   - ◦ Virtual leadership
   - ◦ Digital relationship building
   - ◦ Remote value creation

Strategic Adaptation

1. **Network Evolution**
   - ◦ Platform diversification
   - ◦ Relationship digitization
   - ◦ Value creation innovation
   - ◦ Impact measurement advancement
2. **Value Proposition Development**
   - ◦ Future-focused offerings
   - ◦ Digital value creation
   - ◦ Virtual collaboration
   - ◦ Remote relationship building

Emerging Social Capital Paradigms

New Value Systems

1. **Purpose-Driven Networks**
   - Social impact focus
   - Sustainability alignment
   - Value-based collaboration
   - Mission-driven relationships
2. **Digital Trust Networks**
   - Verified relationships
   - Blockchain trust systems
   - Reputation protocols
   - Smart trust frameworks

Evolving Relationship Models

1. **Hybrid Relationships**
   - Physical-digital integration
   - Mixed reality interaction
   - Blended networking
   - Multi-channel engagement
2. **Community-Centric Networks**
   - Distributed value creation
   - Collective impact
   - Shared resources
   - Collaborative growth

Future Challenges and Opportunities

Emerging Challenges

1. **Digital Divide**
   - Technology access gaps
   - Skill disparities
   - Platform fragmentation
   - Integration challenges
2. **Trust and Privacy**

- ◦ Data protection
- ◦ Digital identity
- ◦ Relationship security
- ◦ Value verification

Future Opportunities

1. **Innovation Spaces**
   - ◦ New relationship models
   - ◦ Value creation platforms
   - ◦ Collaboration systems
   - ◦ Impact measurement tools
2. **Market Evolution**
   - ◦ Emerging sectors
   - ◦ New value propositions
   - ◦ Digital transformation
   - ◦ Global integration

Preparing Your Network for the Future

Strategic Planning

1. **Future-Ready Assessment**
   - ◦ Current state analysis
   - ◦ Gap identification
   - ◦ Technology readiness
   - ◦ Skill evaluation
2. **Development Roadmap**
   - ◦ Capability building
   - ◦ Technology adoption
   - ◦ Relationship evolution
   - ◦ Value creation innovation

Implementation Framework

1. **Transition Planning**
   - ◦ Phase-based evolution
   - ◦ Resource allocation

- Risk management
- Progress measurement

2. **Success Metrics**
   - Adaptation indicators
   - Value creation measures
   - Impact assessment
   - Growth tracking

Action Steps for Future Readiness

1. **Technology Integration**
   - Platform adoption
   - Tool implementation
   - Process digitization
   - Analytics development
2. **Skill Development**
   - Digital capability building
   - Future skill acquisition
   - Continuous learning
   - Adaptation training
3. **Network Evolution**
   - Relationship digitization
   - Value proposition development
   - Platform diversification
   - Impact measurement advancement

Looking Ahead: My Predictions

Short-Term (1-3 Years)

- Increased virtual networking adoption
- CRM (contact relationships management) tools will become more broadly known as RM (relationship management) systems as new features become available
- AI-enhanced relationship management
- Blockchain trust systems emergence

- Mixed reality collaboration growth

Medium-Term (3-5 Years)

- Decentralized network dominance
- Advanced AI relationship optimization
- Immersive networking environments
- Global value creation platforms

Long-Term (5+ Years)

- Quantum networking capabilities
- Neural network integration
- Autonomous relationship management
- Universal value exchange systems

Remember that while technology and social structures continue to evolve, the fundamental principles of authentic relationship building remain constant. Success in the future of social capital will come from balancing technological advancement with human connection, ensuring that innovation serves to enhance rather than replace genuine relationship value.

Conclusion: A Superconnector's Journey

I never could have imagined that it would all start with Detroit techno. There I was, surrounded by all of those electronic sounds and samples, unknowingly learning my first lessons about bringing different elements together. Who would have thought those late nights mixing tracks would teach me so much about mixing people and opportunities?

The journey from there has been anything but linear. One day I'm making electronic music that wins a UK Urban Music Award, moments later I'm spending 11 years at Apple learning how massive products are launched, and then somehow I end up writing copy about surgical robots. It sounds random, but there's a thread running through it all— this knack for seeing how different pieces can fit together to create something new.

What really gets me excited is watching connections spark into something bigger. Like when I helped one of my favorite luxury hotels in Japan develop their musical identity for an ad campaign, or when I had the chance to work with the UN connecting entrepreneurs with radio broadcast tech resources across developing nations. These weren't just projects or introductions—they were opportunities to create ripple effects that went way beyond the initial connection.

I've learned that being a superconnector isn't about having the biggest contact list or being the loudest person in the room. Sometimes it's just about paying attention when someone mentions a challenge and remembering that conversation you had last week with someone who might have the solution. It's about being genuinely curious about people and the problems they're trying to solve.

Surprisingly, the most satisfying moments aren't the big deals (though those are nice too). It's the messages I get months later: "Remember that person you introduced me to? Well, you'll never believe what happened..." Those are the moments that remind me why I love doing this.

Sure, technology has changed how we connect—my old Palm Treo would get a laugh or three these days. But whether I'm attending a friend's event in Hong Kong or meeting up with traveling marketing execs in a swank New York lounge, the fundamentals haven't changed. People still want to work with people they trust, and there's still no replacement for genuine relationships.

Looking back, every environment has taught me something different about connecting people. Sometimes it's about patience, sometimes it's about timing, and sometimes it's just about getting out of the way and letting good people find their own rhythm together.

I've made plenty of mistakes along the way, had my share of connections that didn't quite click, and learned that not every introduction needs to be made. But that's part of the journey too. Each misstep taught me something about doing it better the next time.

If there's one thing I hope readers take from this book, it's that you don't need to be born with some special talent to be good at connecting people. You just need to be genuinely interested in others and willing to pay attention to the possibilities around you. The rest tends to fall into place naturally.

Every day, I'm still learning, still seeing new ways to bring people together, still getting excited about the potential in unexpected connections. That's the real joy of this work. There's always another possibility around the corner, another chance to help good people find each other and create something amazing together.

About The Author

Greg Graham understands the currency of relationships because he's built his career on it. From Detroit's electronic music scene to Silicon Valley, and from the United Nations to medical technology innovation, his journey demonstrates how authentic connections can transcend industries, cultures, and continents.

Beginning in Detroit's vibrant electronic music scene, Greg's early career led him to London, where his talent for building meaningful relationships helped him thrive in the competitive entertainment landscape. His UK Urban Music Award and campaign collaborations with artists like Pharrell Williams while managing music promotion for Promo Only validated his relationship-centric approach to business. His next chapter in Miami further expanded his network in the music industry through his project, Comfort Crusade, crafting sophisticated electronic soundscapes designed for those seeking refuge from mainstream music—the perfect accompaniment for moments of solitude in luxury hotel resorts or during reflective solo travels.

During his eleven-year tenure at Apple in Miami and New York, Greg mastered the art of orchestrating complex projects and building cross-functional relationships. This experience proved invaluable when he took on a summer role at the United Nations while still at Apple, where he developed digital platforms connecting entrepreneurs in developing nations with global resources and opportunities.

Following his time at Apple, Greg launched his freelance copywriting venture, Greg Writes Well, demonstrating how relationship currency could help establish a successful independent business. This led to his role at Intuitive Surgical, where his talent for building trust and understanding helped him transform complex technical concepts into compelling narratives for their surgical robotics technology.

Today, as director of Carmine Street Media, Greg has developed what he calls the "producer mindset"—a revolutionary approach to business that combines relationship building with people and technology. This mindset, shaped by his diverse career experiences, represents the ability to bring together seemingly disparate elements—whether they're people, ideas, or technologies—to create something greater than the sum of its parts. His company's unique blend of original music composition, strategic copywriting, and AI integration reflects this philosophy, helping organizations build meaningful connections with their audiences.

Identified by Gallup as having "Woo" as a signature strength, Greg's natural ability to build positive, collaborative environments has been consistently recognized by colleagues and clients worldwide. However, he maintains that relationship building is not just an innate talent but a skill that can be learned, refined, and strategically leveraged—a philosophy that forms the foundation of this book.

Drawing from experiences spanning five continents and multiple industries, Greg offers readers more than just theory. He provides a practical framework for understanding how relationships function as another form of global currency, and more importantly, how to ethically build and maintain relationship wealth that creates value for all parties involved.

In *Relationships Are Currency*, Greg shares the strategies and insights that have enabled him to successfully navigate diverse professional landscapes, showing how the producer mindset can help anyone build and leverage meaningful relationships in today's global economy.

The End
Thank you for reading.

I intend to help you grow your work connections, expand your support network, and nurture relationships with the people who are truly in your corner.

More of my career topic books available as ebooks

www.ingramcontent.com/pod-product-compliance
Lightning Source LLC
Chambersburg PA
CBHW070115230526
45472CB00004B/1265